D1193796

CONSERVATION OF
ENDANGERED SPECIES

SOUTH LAKETOWN LIBRARY

SAVING THE ENDANGERED
BLUE WHALE

SIMONE PAYMENT

Britannica®
Educational Publishing

IN ASSOCIATION WITH

ROSEN
EDUCATIONAL SERVICES

Published in 2016 by Britannica Educational Publishing (a trademark of Encyclopædia Britannica, Inc.) in association with The Rosen Publishing Group, Inc.
29 East 21st Street, New York, NY 10010

Copyright © 2016 The Rosen Publishing Group, Inc. and Encyclopaedia Britannica, Inc. Encyclopaedia Britannica, Britannica, and the Thistle logo are registered trademarks of Encyclopædia Britannica, Inc. All rights reserved.

Distributed exclusively by Rosen Publishing.
To see additional Britannica Educational Publishing titles, go to rosenpublishing.com.

First Edition

Britannica Educational Publishing
J.E. Luebering: Director, Core Reference Group
Mary Rose McCudden: Editor, Britannica Student Encyclopedia

Rosen Publishing
Nicholas Croce: Editor
Nelson Sá: Art Director
Michael Moy: Designer
Cindy Reiman: Photography Manager
Sherri Jackson: Photo Researcher

Library of Congress Cataloging-in-Publication Data

Payment, Simone.
Saving the endangered blue whale / Simone Payment.
    pages cm. — (Conservation of endangered species)
Includes bibliographical references and index.
Audience: Grades 1 to 4.
ISBN 978-1-68048-247-8 (library bound) — ISBN 978-1-5081-0052-2 (pbk.) — ISBN 978-1-68048-305-5 (6-pack)
1. Blue whale—Juvenile literature. 2. Blue whale—Conservation—Juvenile literature. I. Title.

QL737.C424P376 2015
599.5'248—dc23

2015016639

Manufactured in the United States of America

Photo Credits: Cover Seb c'est bien/Shutterstock.com; back cover, p. 1, interior pages background Godruma/Shutterstock.com; p. 4 Tagstock1/Shutterstock.com; p. 5 © National Geographic Image Collection/Alamy; p. 6 Encyclopaedia Britannica/Universal Images Group/Getty Images; p. 7 Fotosearch/Getty Images; p. 8 Mark Carwardine/Photolibrary/Getty Images; p. 9 © FLPA/Malcolm Schuyl/age fotostock; p. 10 David Fleetham/Perspectives/Getty Images; p. 11 © Nature Picture Library/Alamy; p. 12 © Cranston, Bob/Animals Animals; p. 13 Auscape/Universal Images Group/Getty Images; p. 14 SCIEPRO/Science Photo Library/Getty Images; p. 15 AguaSonic Acoustics/Science Source; p. 16 melissaf84/Shutterstock.com; p. 17 iStockphoto.com/MR1805; p. 18 Marka/Universal Images Group/Getty Images; p. 19 nito/Shutterstock.com; p. 20 © Galen Rowell/Mountain Light/Alamy; p. 21 kojihirano/Shutterstock.com; p. 22 De Agostini/A. Dagli Orti/Getty Images; p. 23 Olga Pink/Shutterstock.com; p. 24 papa1266/iStock/Thinkstock; p. 25 Wyatt Rivard/Shutterstock.com; p. 26 © Francois Gohier/VWPics/age fotostock; p. 27 Flip Nicklin/Minden Pictures/Getty Images; p. 28 nui7711/Shutterstock.com; p. 29 Mark Conlin/Oxford Scientific/Getty Images; cover and interior pages design elements Aliaksei_7799/Shutterstock.com (whale graphic), Ethan Daniels/Shutterstock.com (whale skin)

CONTENTS

THE ENDANGERED BLUE WHALE

The blue whale is the largest animal on Earth. In fact, it is likely the largest animal that has ever lived. Like all whales, it is a **mammal**. About every ten to twenty minutes, it must come to the surface to breathe.

Blue whales live in all oceans on Earth. There used to be more than two hundred thousand blue whales on the planet. However, for many years, blue whales were hunted for their oil and body parts. They were

The blue whale is larger than any other animal on Earth.

Vocabulary

Mammals **are warm-blooded animals that breathe air, have a spine, and feed their young with milk produced by the mother.**

close to extinction in the 1960s, when laws were passed to protect them. Today the blue whale remains an endangered species. Scientists and conservationists are working to study these huge animals and to help them survive.

Before laws were made to limit whale hunting, people hunted many types of whales, like this sperm whale.

PHYSICAL FEATURES OF THE BLUE WHALE

Ablue whale may be more than 100 feet (30 meters) long. This is about the length of three school buses. Females are usually longer than males.

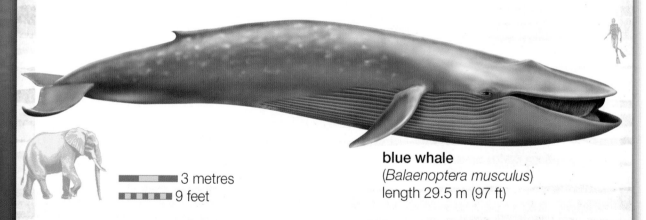

3 metres
9 feet

blue whale
(*Balaenoptera musculus*)
length 29.5 m (97 ft)

An elephant and a human look tiny when they are compared to the enormous blue whale.

Think About It

The adult blue whale has no natural predator. What might be a reason for this?

Blue whales can weigh 150 tons or more. That means one blue whale may be heavier than thirty elephants. Just the heart of one blue whale can weigh about 1,500 pounds (700 kilograms).

The blue whale's body is blue-gray in color with some white or lighter gray areas. The animals' bellies are white but sometimes look yellowish. The yellow color comes from the thousands of tiny yellowish-green creatures that live on the skin of a blue whale.

Blue whales have smooth, flexible skin and flat heads. Their slippery skin and long shape help them glide through the water.

Near a blue whale's mouth are grooves called ventral pleats. The pleats let the mouth stretch widely as the whale eats.

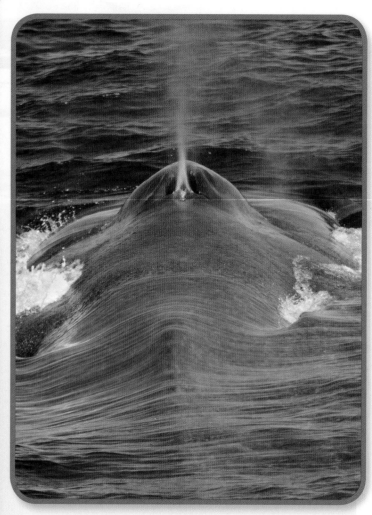

A blue whale's two blowholes are protected by a large splashguard, which helps keep water out.

On the top of their heads, blue whales have blowholes. These are two holes similar to nostrils. They allow the whale to breathe when it comes to the surface of the water.

Blue whales have a strong tail with two curved flat sections called flukes. They have a small fin at the top of their back near the tail. They also have two flippers on their chest, called pectoral flippers. Blue whales use their tails for swimming and diving. Their flippers are mostly for steering or for slowing down.

On the blue whale's throat and chest are eighty to one hundred long grooves. The grooves let the whale's mouth stretch widely. Instead of teeth, the mouth contains a structure called baleen. The baleen has bristles that trap small **prey**.

Vocabulary

Prey **are animals hunted or killed by another animal for food.**

About three hundred baleen plates hang from a blue whale's top jaw. Baleen is made of a protein called keratin, also found in human hair.

WHERE BLUE WHALES LIVE

Blue whales often travel thousands of miles during the year.

Blue whales are found in all the world's oceans. Some live in the northern Pacific and Atlantic oceans. Others live around Antarctica. There are more blue whales in southern oceans than in northern areas.

Many blue whales travel during the year. For example, in the summer they may feed in cold waters near the North or

Think About It

Most blue whales travel long distances every year. Which parts of a blue whale's body help it to travel?

South Pole. Then, in the winter they may move to warmer waters to mate. Some blue whales live all year round in the same place.

Because blue whales often dive deep below the surface to feed, they usually stay in deeper water. But sometimes they come closer to coastal areas to feed in the shallower waters.

Blue whales usually feed at depths of up to 300 feet (100 m).

WHAT ARE BLUE WHALES' LIVES LIKE?

Blue whales live alone or in small groups. They can travel as fast as 20 miles (32 kilometers) or more per hour. They must come to the surface of the water for air every ten to twenty minutes. The blow of a blue whale is the air, water, and mucus it spouts when it comes to the surface.

Whales do not sleep deeply like humans do. They need to keep part of their

After a dive, a blue whale will blow eight to fifteen times. These spouts can be as high as 33 feet (10 m).

Think About It

After a feeding season, blue whales can go without eating for months. How can blue whales survive so long without food?

brain awake in order to take a breath. Whales rest half of their brain at a time, taking very short naps near the water's surface.

Blue whales feast on many tiny shrimplike creatures called krill. First they take in a huge mouthful of water. Then they use their enormous tongues to push the water out through their baleen plates. The baleen traps thousands of tiny krill that the whale then swallows.

A single adult whale can swallow several tons of krill each day.

BLUE WHALE COMMUNICATION

Sound travels about five times faster in water than it does in air. This may be why blue whales use sound for survival.

Blue whales have excellent hearing. They can hear sounds that the human ear cannot. Blue whales can also make sounds, such as clicks and low noises, that only other whales can hear.

Scientists think that a blue whale may produce certain sounds to attract a mate.

Compare and Contrast

Noise from ships and other underwater machines has increased greatly over the last one hundred years. How has this changed the way blue whales hear and communicate?

The blue whale is also the loudest animal on the planet! It is even louder than a jet engine. It can make noises that travel thousands of miles underwater. Scientists think that blue whales communicate to find one another, to help each other find food, or to find a new mate.

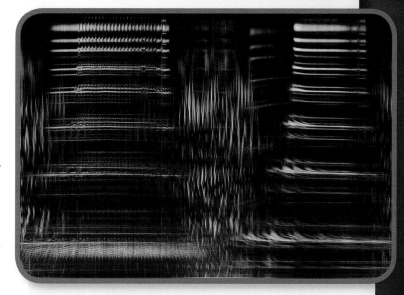

The loud, low noises that whales make are called songs. This photo shows a whale song in graph form.

THE BLUE WHALE LIFE CYCLE

Blue whale calves stay with their mothers for about the first year of their lives.

About one year after mating, a female blue whale gives birth to one baby, called a calf. The newborn whale is about 25 feet (8 m) long. Newborns already weigh about 6,000 pounds (2,700 kg).

A calf can drink 100 gallons (380 liters) of its mother's rich milk a day. This helps it gain 200 pounds (90 kg) and grow more than 1 inch (2.5 centimeters) every day.

Vocabulary

Krill are tiny shrimplike animals that live in the ocean. They belong to the group of animals called crustaceans.

Calves can swim from the moment they are born. They spend the first several months of their lives in warmer ocean water. When a blue whale calf is about six months old, it will begin to feed on krill and travel on its own.

Blue whales become fully mature adults between the ages of six to ten years. They can usually live for about eighty to ninety years.

Blue whale calves nurse on their mother's milk for at least the first six months of life.

WHAT IS AN ENDANGERED SPECIES?

An endangered species is any type of plant or animal that is in danger of disappearing forever. If a species, or type, of plant or animal dies out completely, it becomes extinct. Animals and plants depend on each other and on their environment to survive. When their environment, or habitat, changes or is

Some whales wash ashore after being killed by ships. This blue whale washed up on a beach.

Think About It

When humans bring a new species of plant or animal to an environment, it can endanger an animal or plant already living in that environment. What are some reasons that might happen?

destroyed, plants and animals may not be able to survive. They then become endangered.

Natural disasters or changes in the climate can harm or destroy habitats. Humans pollute habitats with garbage, car fumes, and factory wastes. Humans destroy habitats by clearing land for roads, buildings, and farms. They also may hunt and kill too many of certain types of animals.

Though some of the garbage in the ocean comes to shore, much of it floats in the ocean.

PROTECTING ENDANGERED SPECIES

In the 1960s, people became aware that many species were endangered. Today, many countries have made it illegal to harm, capture, kill, or sell endangered species. In addition, many organizations work to keep endangered species from becoming extinct.

The International Union for Conservation of Nature keeps lists of

Before the 1966 ban on whaling, many whale species were endangered.

Compare and Contrast

Humans can help animals that live on land increase their population. Why might it be harder for humans to help endangered sea creatures like blue whales do the same?

endangered species. The Nature Conservancy and the World Wildlife Fund help to set aside land for threatened wildlife.

Nature preserves and zoos help endangered animals to reproduce. Such programs have helped to increase the populations of the black-footed ferret, the California condor, and other endangered animals.

In 1982, the total California condor population was just twenty-two. However, its population has increased since it was put on the endangered species list.

WHY IS THE BLUE WHALE AN ENDANGERED SPECIES?

As whaling equipment and ships improved, many more whales were killed.

In the 1800s, people began hunting whales in large numbers for their meat, bones, **blubber**, and baleen. The blubber was boiled and turned into oil that was used for cooking or as fuel in lamps.

During the 1930–1931 whaling season, as many as 29,000 blue whales were killed. Scientists believe humans killed 350,000 blue

Vocabulary

Blubber **is the layer of fat found underneath a whale's skin.**

whales during the years that whales were hunted. Then in 1966, the International Whaling Commission made it illegal to kill blue whales. In 1986, the organization limited the hunting of all types of whales. However, a few countries continue to hunt whales.

Scientists are not sure of the exact population of blue whales. However, they believe today there are between 10,000 and 25,000 in the world. Blue whales are still an endangered species.

Before electricity, many people used oil lamps for light. Whale blubber could be turned into oil for these lamps.

Although blue whales are now protected from whaling, they face other problems. Blue whales are sometimes hit by large ships and either injured or killed. They also can become tangled in fishing gear that is left behind in the ocean. This can slow them down or cut their skin and cause infections, making them sick.

Large ships often hit whales. Sometimes whales die from the injuries caused by these ships.

Climate change also affects whales. The world's oceans are growing warmer. The krill that whales rely on as a food source can live only in cooler water. With less krill in the ocean, blue whales will have less to eat.

Compare and Contrast

Animals living in any environment can face problems from pollution. What are some examples of pollution that can be especially harmful to ocean animals?

Pollution in the ocean, such as garbage and chemicals, can kill whales. Chemicals can build up in a whale's blubber and harm it slowly. Noise pollution from ships can change how whales hear and communicate.

Rising sea levels from melting polar ice caps will affect people and animals on land, as well as those creatures living in the world's oceans.

WHAT IS BEING DONE TO HELP BLUE WHALES?

The International Whaling Commission is in charge of protecting all whales. It enforces the laws against whaling. It is working to stop any country from continuing to hunt whales. It also works with conservation groups to try to improve the condition of the world's oceans.

In the waters around Antarctica and throughout

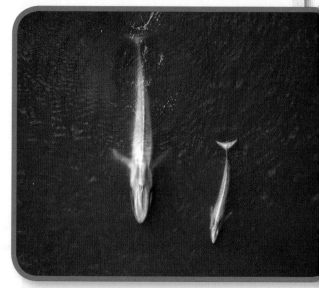

Australia has set up a sanctuary in the waters off its coast. Hawaii established a whale sanctuary for humpback whales.

Vocabulary

Sanctuaries are places that provide shelter or protection.

the Indian Ocean, there are whale **sanctuaries**. In these protected areas, blue whales are less likely to be hit by ships.

Scientists are also studying blue whales to find ways to better protect them and help increase their population. Scientists have tagged some blue whales with devices that send out signals. These signals tell scientists where the blue whales travel so they can learn more about the lives of the animals.

This blue whale was tagged with a satellite tracker in the Santa Barbara Channel off the coast of California.

CONCLUSION

People can work together to clean up trash that is already in our oceans.

Everyone can play a part in helping blue whales to thrive. Things humans do can have a big effect on the plants and animals that share our world. Here are a few things everyone can do: Help keep the world's oceans clean by not polluting. Conserve energy to slow down global warming so the ocean will stay at the right temperature for whales and their food sources. Join a conservation group that works to stop

Think About It

Whales have just one baby at a time, and they have a baby every two or three years. How do you think these two facts affect how quickly the blue whale population can increase?

whaling and help clean the oceans.

Blue whales are the largest creatures ever to have lived on Earth, and they have been around for a very long time. If humans help keep them safe and keep their environment clean, perhaps they will be around for many more years to come.

Some populations of blue whales are recovering, but there is still much work to be done.

GLOSSARY

BRISTLE A short stiff hair or something like a hair.

CLIMATE The weather found in a certain place over a long period of time.

CONSERVATIONIST A person who works to protect things found in nature.

FUEL A material used to produce heat or power by burning.

FUME A disagreeable smoke or gas.

GROOVE A long, narrow channel made in a surface.

HABITAT The place or type of place where a plant or animal naturally or normally lives or grows.

INFECTION An illness caused by a germ or parasite.

NATURE PRESERVE Area set aside to protect plants and animals.

PECTORAL Located in, near, or on the chest.

POLLUTE To damage nature with waste made by humans.

POPULATION A group of one or more species of organisms living in a particular area or habitat.

PREDATOR An animal that obtains food mostly by killing and eating other animals.

PROCESS To take in information and organize it for use in a variety of ways.

SPECIES A group of plants or animals of the same kind and with the same name.

THRIVE To do well or grow in number.

FOR MORE INFORMATION

Books

Baillie, Marilyn, and Jonathan Baillie. *How to Save a Species*. Toronto, ON: Owlkids Books, 2014.

Bjorklund, Ruth. *Blue Whales*. New York: Children's Press, 2014.

Desmond, Jenni. *The Blue Whale*. Brooklyn, NY: Enchanted Lion Books, 2015.

Harris, Caroline. *Discover Science: Whales and Dolphins*. New York: Kingfisher, 2010.

Hutchison, Patricia. *Blue Whales*. North Mankato, MN: Child's World, 2015.

Siebert, Charles. *The Secret World of Whales*. San Francisco, CA: Chronicle Books, 2011.

Websites

Because of the changing nature of Internet links, Rosen Publishing has developed an online list of websites related to the subject of this book. This site is updated regularly. Please use this link to access this list:

http://www.rosenlinks.com/CONS/Whale

INDEX

SAND LAKE TOWN LIBRARY

Sand Lake Town Library

3 8129 00040 3801

APR 1 6 ENT'D

DATE DUE